T0065454

OVER 100 EASY THINGS

YOU CAN DO

TO PLEASE OUR HEAVENLY ABBA

GOD ALMIGHTY

FOREVER IN YAHSHUA

(JESUS) NAME

IF THE LORD WILL IF
WE SHALL LIVE WE SHALL
DO THIS OR THAT.. AMEN

SISTER PATRICIA INEZ SANDIFER

WESTBOW
PRESS®
A DIVISION OF THOMAS NELSON
& ZONDERVAN

This book is a work of non-fiction. Unless otherwise noted, the author and the publisher make no explicit guarantees as to the accuracy of the information contained in this book and in some cases, names of people and places have been altered to protect their privacy.

WestBow Press books may be ordered through booksellers or by contacting:

WestBow Press
A Division of Thomas Nelson & Zondervan
1663 Liberty Drive
Bloomington, IN 47403
www.westbowpress.com
844-714-3454

Interior Image Credit: Ted Brown and the Sandifers

All Scripture quotations are taken from the King James Version.

ISBN: 978-1-6642-0253-5 (sc)
ISBN: 978-1-6642-0252-8 (hc)
ISBN: 978-1-6642-0254-2 (e)

Library of Congress Control Number: 2020915700

Print information available on the last page.

WestBow Press rev. date: 04/13/2022

INTRODUCTION

This book is wrote to encourage you to never stop living the
way God Almighty and Jesus Christ say live

Read the bible day and night with your family

Pray evening morning and at noon, with your family

Tithe, you and your family

Search the scriptures to know what the bible say do for yourself.
That way you will know the truth. And teach your children and
grandchildren and great grandchildren

Peace Be Unto You.

God Almighty and Jesus Christ put us here to have mercy.

Do not take all of people taxes for no reason for child support ect. People got to live.

Do not take people driving privillages have mercy. People can use mercy. Because they do not pay their child support. Just garnish their check for child support.

It is not just that prisoners in prisons are not paid decent money. Where your compassion. Do right by all prisoners. And get them windows fixed in prisons and jails. And give them skills whiles they in prisons. For good permant jobs when they are released. You know they need homes. Build homes instead of prisons.

Give all prisoners including prisoners with drug felonies

   (a) section 8
   (b) food stamps
   (c) medicade
   (d) jobs
   (e) And let them live with people in low income housing and section 8, whenever they need to. If they want to live with loved ones with section 8 and low income housing. Let them. That will please God. People still love the prisoner. And want them at home once they are released.

Dedication

PSALMS 70 Verse 4

The Authorize KING JAMES Version
Holy Bible

Let all those that seek thee rejoice and be glad in thee and let such as love thy salvation say continually, let God be magnified.

AMEN

LUKE 10:25-27

And, behold, a certain lawyer stood up, and tempted him saying Master, what shall I do to inherit eternal life? He said unto him, What is written in the law? How readest thou

And he answering said, Thou shalt love the Lord thy God with all thy heart, and with all thy soul, and with all thy strength, and with all thy mind; and thy neighbour as thyself.

PSALMS 34 Verse 1

I will bless the LORD at all times: his praise shall continually be in my mouth.

PSALMS 84 Verses 4 and 10

The Authorize KING JAMES Version Holy Bible

Blessed are they that dwell in thy house - they will be still praising thee. Selah

For a day in thy courts is better than a thousand. I had rather be a doorkeeper in the house of my God than to dwell in the tents of wickness.

PSALMS 92 Verses 13-14

Those that be planted in the house of the LORD shall flourish in the courts of our God

They shall bring forth fruit in old age; they shall be fat and flourishing.

AMEN

PSALMS 82 Verse 6

THE AUTHORIZE KING JAMES VERSION
Holy Bible

I have said, ye are gods; and all of you are children of the Most High. Amen

In Yahshua name the one and only True Wise Blessed living Saviour and Messiah and Son of God. Jesus died on the cross and rose from the dead with all power in his hands. No matter how Great Jesus is. No matter how old Jesus is. Jesus Honour God Almighty. No matter what Jesus went through.

We the children of the highest thank, love, bless, honour, fear you Abba and obey God Almighty and "Yahshua" (Jesus) Hamashiac (Christ)

True Messiah. Forever. Amen

Dedication of Book.

This book is dedicated to our Heavenley Abba and Saviour. The one and only True living Blessed living God and Saviour and Messiah that live and that will ever live. Elshaddi God Almighty Elohim (God) I am that I am Rev. Holy, Master Rabbi. God Almighty and Jesus Christ

To our Blessed Parents that God and Jesus taught to train us up in the way we should go. So when we is old we will not depart. To our parents that never put us out because we were 18yr old or grown. To our parents that chased us bedtimes. To our parents that would not let up off you. They talk to you until you got it right. And lived like God said live. Everyday no matter how grown we were. Our parents told us who to be around and who not to be around. And so on. Mr. & Mrs. Clifton and Clearce Sandifer Sr. Born and raised in Jackson and Mc Comb Miss. And lived in Gary Ind where they trained us to live for God by reading that bible and living it before us. And teaching us 7 children what they learned.

To The Children of the Most High God. My (4) dear children and 19 dear grandchildren and dear great grandchildren Latasha Hendrix (Johnson) Janel Johnson Timothy Sandifer III Reginald Sandifer Sr. and their family. To Kenneth Johnson Latarsha husband. Latarshas sons Kenneth, Kendall, Eric & children, Breanad children. Janels husband David Johnson. Janel children Alize Smith (Stanley) Garrette Smith Stanley, Yasha Johson. David Johnson & family Timothy Johnson

Timothy children. Timothy Sandifer IV Brandon Sandifer, Cherish Sandifer Cardea

Reginald Children Reginald Jr Reginea Sandifer Rakeal Sandifer

To the poor needy just unjust rich blacks, Isralite, Jews, Gentiles whites Japanese, Chinise all colors, relegion race, creations and to Mr. Eric Shroder from my Publishing Company and the entire patient loving understanding kind publishing company that published this book with God and Jesus help. And to Elisha at my church Israel The Church of Jesus, and The Commandment Keepers with Habakkuk, Boie, Danny, Marlon all you Sabbath Day Keepers out there.

To the children of the highest. The repenting dear prisoners.

To my 3 brothers 2 sisters and their families.

(Glenn) & Sandra & family
(Wilton Sandifer Sr) & family
(Ira) & Felicia and Cat
(Mildred Sease) & Willie Sease & family
(Mary Sandifer), Bernadine Alexzander Cannie, Luella and family & friends who truley stood by her when her son Antione Lemonte Howard was gunned down in his home.

To my nephew Antione and the loving church that was there for him loving him enough to give him the Gospel of God. And to the Preaching Most Blessed City I know Gary Ind & all of Marshalltown Terrace in Gary Ind.

Praise the LORD

Gary Indiana and all Gary Ind, Hammond and Chicago Churches that invited me and my (4) dear children to church.

We was looking for God and Jesus so we went to every church that invited us.

Praise the LORD Marshalltown Terrace, New Mount Marioh Pastor & Mrs. Reed. God will never forget none of you God bless you all rich & poor. God bless America. (NEHEMIAH 10:35)

Amen

Remember to feed yourself and animals and all God Almighty creations clean foods - we ought to obey God rather than man.

Read.

LEVITICUS 3:17
LEVITICUS 7
LEVITICUS 17
DEUTERONOMY 14

The authorize KING JAMES version Holy Bible

God Almighty & Jesus Christ Bless you. Thank you. Thank you.

God wish that all would be saved and come to the knowledge of the truth.

Make sure you pray for the people you tell about God word.

I wish what God and Jesus wish.

Amen.

Do this. Winter, spring, summer fall
Set up tables and talk to the poor needy homeless gangs ect about GOD word outdoors. In the winter get those tin can put charcol in them to stay warm, and feed them chilli soup, stew in the winter fried chicken juice koolaid. And bibles.

Amen.

Read God word for yourself and with your family children neighbours, coworkers church members poor needy homeless, gangs prisoners, teachers ect. Authorties rich & poor.

Over 100 different things you can do to please God Almighty forever
(In Yahshua name)#
Jesus

1st Book

Over 100 easy things you can do to (please God Almighty) forever
"(In Yahshua Name)"
        Jesus

If the LORD will we shall live we shall do this or that

MATTHEW 4
Verse 17

(1)   From that time Jesus began to preach and say, Repent for the Kingdom of heaven is at hand.

Repent and tell the Father God Almighty how sorry you is for sinning. Whoever else you need to say you are sorry to call them up and say you are sorry. Or write. If they won't listen DO NOT call back. Don't force them to hear. MATTHEW 5 Verse 44

(2) But I say unto you, love your enemies, bless them that curse you, do good to them that hate you, and pray for them which despitefully use you, and persecute you. Obey the word here.

(3) Next say Jesus is LORD say Jesus is THE SON OF GOD that died on the cross and rose from the dead with all power in his hand. For rich and poor to have God Almighty Hope, Plan and future. Amen

(4) Say Jesus Christ is and always will be the only TRUE LIVING Son of God, Savior, and Messiah.

(5) Ask The Father God Almighty will he let his will be done for you your family, kinfolks, friends neibhors, church, all creations forever "(In Yahshua Name)". If the LORD will if we shall live we shall live we shall do this a that. Amen

(6) PROVERBS 25 Verses 21-22

If thine enemy be hungry give him bread to eat; and if he be thirsty, give him water to drink.

(7) For thou shalt heap coals of fire upon his head, and the LORD shall reward thee.

(8)   MATTHEW 14:23

And when he had sent the multitudes away, he went up into a mountain apart to pray: and when the evening was came, he was there alone.

(9)   PSALMS 55: Verse 17

Evening and morning, and at noon, will I pray and cry aloud and he shall hear my voice

(10)   MARK 1: Verse 35

And in the morning rising up a great while before day, he went out, and departed into a solitary place and there prayed

So pray evening, morning and at noon.

(11)   LUKE 22 Verse 41

And he was withdrawn, from them about a stone's cast, and kneeled down and prayed.

(12)   LUKE 6:12

And it came to pass in those days, that he went out into a mountain to pray, and continued all night in prayer to God

(13) PSALM 5 Verse 7

But as for me, I will come into thy house in the multitude of thy mercy: and in thy fear will I worship toward thy holy temple.

Pray (facing the east) at all times.

(14) 1 CORINTHIANS 11 Verses 4-5

Every man praying or prophesying, having his head covered dishonoureth his head

But every woman that prayeth or prophesieth with her head uncovered dishonoureth her head: for that is even all one as if she were shove.

Males (never) cover your head when you pray or prophesy.

Females (always) cover your head when you pray or prophesy.

(15) Now go gather you precious family and pray. If you like you can pray 3:00, 6:00 9:00 or 12 noon. Or pray when it is convient for you. Read the Book of Act together with your family before bedtime.

(16) Read MATTHEW Chapter 6 when you pray. And if you have anything else you would like to talk to God about. Pray that so no one will hear.

* If you have someone over 18 that do not want to pray. "Dont force them." Pray for them and their generations and kinfolks. They have rights to choose. Amen

(17) EPHESIANS 5 Verse 8

For ye were sometimes darkness, but now are ye light in the LORD: Walk as children of light. We made mistakes so pray for the next person.

(18) JOSHUA 1 Verse 8

This book of the Law shall not depart out of thy mouth: but thou shalt meditate therein day and night, that thou mayest observe to do according to all that is written therein for then thou shalt make thy way prosperous and then thou shalt have good success.

If someone come to me with a problem. The first thing I say is LORD what would you have Jesus to do. All the answers are in the Holy Bible to everybody problems. Get <u>THE AUTHORIZE KING JAMES VERSION HOLY BIBLE.</u> Amen

(19) 1 PETER 2 Verse 21

For even hereunto were ye called: because Christ also suffered for us, leaving us an example that ye shall follow his steps. Amen.

God Almighty promised the same work and greater works "(Yahshua)" Jesus did. We will do. So let's give to the poor including felon prisoners.

And let's stop all this fussing and fighting, cusshing, scratching and snatching, slapping. And let's start repenting and live a holy saved life.

(20) EPHESIANS 5 Verse 1

Be ye therefore followers of God, as dear children.

Amen

(21) EPHESIANS 3 Verse 20

Now unto him that is able to do exceeding abundantly above all that we ask or think, according to the power that worketh in us.

"(There is not one thing)" nowhere too hard for God or Jesus. They wish all would be saved, and came to the knowlege of the truth. "Call God and Jesus and talk to them even when everything is alright. Let them know how much you love them and can't wait to see their face. Amen

(22) COLOSSIANS 3 Verse 2

Set you affection on things above, not on things on the earth. Amen.

Spend your time repenting, praying, reading, studing THE WORD OF GOD taking care of your house (your) family. Give to the poor. Go to church or have church at home. Hear God WORD on the computer every week.

    (a) Wed: 9:00 p.m (Gary Ind time)
    (b) Fridays 9:00 pm (Gary Ind time)
    (c) Saturday 1:00 pm (Gary Ind time)

Go to …

www.Thykingdomcome7.com

You will be so very glad you did. Tell all your family and kinfolks, neibhors and friends to hear and obey God word too.

Every week. Same time every week. The phone number to get the address to the church is (219) 979-2633 *Brother Elisha (Pastor)

(23) (23) COLOSSIANS 4 Verse 6

Let your speech be alway with grace, seasoned with salt that ye may know how ye ought to answer every man. Amen

(24) COLOSSIANS 3 Verse 16

Let the word of Christ dwell in you richly in all wisdom teaching and admonishing one another in Psalms, and hymns and spiritual songs, singing with grace in your hearts to the LORD.

Amen

(25) PROVERBS 31 Verse 26

She openeth her mouth with wisdom; and in her tongue is the law of kindness. Be kind. Amen

(26) PSALMS 39 Verse 1

I said I will take heed to my ways, that I sin not with my tongue: I will keep my mouth with a bridle, while the wicked is before me. Amen

(27) PSALMS 81 Verse 10

I am the LORD thy God which brought thee out of the land of Egypt: Open thy mouth wide, and I will fill it. Amen

Keep your mouth closed when the wicked around just walk away and go home and pray. Tell God Almighty your side of the story. He want to hear from you. Amen

Other than that open your mouth when needed. Just say what will please God Almighty (In Jesus Name). Amen

(28) PSALM 82 Verse 6

I have said, ye are gods; and all of you are children of the Most High. Muslims are the children of the Most High too. It is written. Including Muslims, Buddist, Non believers. So pray right with mercy. Pray for each other relegion race, people family, authorties

(29) LUKE 1 Verse 37

For with God nothing shall be impossible. Amen

It is not impossible for The Most High God to make all people and denomanations one. And he and Jesus know how to make all creations forget how to sin. So pray.

Ask God will he make all creations forever forget how to sin. (In Yahshua Name) Amen

Jesus

If the LORD will if we shall live we shall do this or that. Amen.

(30) Or do you think that is much too hard for God Almighty? Ask the Father God Almighty for the faith of the Lamb of God right now. Amen

(31) JEREMIAH 32 Verse 27

Behold I am the LORD, the God of all flesh: is there any thing too hard for God say no. Amen

(32) LUKE 18 Verse 27

And he said, The things which are impossible with men are possible with God. Amen

Can God Almighty save all creations. Do he know how. Say yes Amen

(33) PHILLIPPIANS 4 Verse 19

But my God shall supply all your need according to his riches in glory by Christ Jesus. Amen

Can God Almighty supply all creations with what they need for God Almighty to put and keep their names in The Lambs Book of Life. And can he supply all our need so he can put us in his kingdom of heaven. Say yes. Yes. Amen

(34) PHILIPPIANS 4 Verse 2

I beseech Eu-o'di-as, and beseech Syn'-ty-che, that they be of the same mind in the LORD. Amen

Get together once a month or once a week. And have dinner at Golden Corroll. And give someone that is poor walking down the street a gift card to eat at Golden Corroll and bus fare. Once a month will be fine. If you can afford to go more than once a month. Make sure you feed the poor also. Start with family!

(35) PROVERBS 29 Verse 7

The righteous considereth the cause of the poor: but the wicked regardeth not to know it. Amen *Consider the cause of the poor. Feed & clothe the poor. Donate to shelters.

(36) PROVERBS 28 Verse 27

He that giveth unto the poor shall not lack: but he that hideth his eyes shall have many a curse. Amen "DO NOT HIDE your eyes.

(37) PROVERBS 22 Verse 16

He that oppresseth the poor to increase his riches and he that giveth to the rich shall surley come to want. Amen

Do not oppress the poor or no one else.

(38) PROVERBS 21 Verse 13

Whoso stoppeth his ears at the cry of the poor, he also shall cry himself, but shall not be heard. Amen

Do-Not-Stop-your-ears of the cry of the poor. Amen Including (Poor Family members).
Do-Not-Stop-your ears from God Almighty word. Amen

(39) PROVERBS 21 Verse 26

He covetheth greedily all the day long; but the righteous giveth and spare not. Amen

Give to the poor and needy including felons. Amen

(40) PROVERBS 19 Verse 17

He that hath pity upon the poor lendeth unto the LORD; and that which he hath given will he pay him again. Amen

Have pity on the poor including felon prisoner. Amen

(41) PROVERBS 16 Verse 24

Pleasant words are as an honeycomb, sweet to the soul and health to the bones. Use pleasant words. Amen

(42) PROVERBS 14 Verse 21

He that despiseth his neighbour sinneth: but he that hath mercy on the poor, happy is he. Amen

Do-not despise no one or nothing. *And do your duty have mercy on the poor (including Felon Prisoners). Amen

(43) PSALMS 69 Verse 33

For the LORD heareth the poor, and despiseth not his prisoners. Amen

Follow Jesus examples forever. Amen

(44) PSALMS 111 Verse 9

He sent redemption unto his people: he hath commanded his covenant for ever: holy and reverend is his name. Amen

-Never-Never-Never call no one Holy or Rev, Rabbi, Master, (also read MATTHEW 23) Amen

(45) JOHN 3 Verse 17

For God sent not his son into the world to condemn the world; but that the world through him might be saved. Amen

-Never-Never-Never-condemn no one or nothing. Amen

(46) MATTHEW 7 Verse 1

Judge not that ye be not judged. Amen

(47) ♥ Thanks LORD

Rebell aganist Satan do not do anything his evil self want you to do. Amen

You need money, husband, wife. A job, a place to live clean foods.

Say Father (In Jesus Name)
As you know I sin. I am a sinner.

So is all my house (family) and kinfolks.

Will you forgive us. And lead us all away from sin? As well as all creations forever?

If God Permit.
If the LORD will if we shall live we shall do this or that.

We need you to show us all how to get saved and stay saved forever. And will you give us enough money to do everything we need to do. Will you give us and all creations forever what they have need of before they and we can ask. According to your riches in glory by Christ Jesus now and forever. And may we all have some of you and "Yahshua" (Jesus) money?
♥ We love you LORD!
If God Permit
If the LORD will if we shall live we shall do this or that. Amen

(48) PSALM 84 Verse 4

Blessed are they that dwell in thy house they will be still praising thee. Selah. Amen

*** I'm on a fixed income right now. Until God
Almighty increase our and my family income.
I give 2.00 per month for offering and 2.00 per
month for the poor. And I give 10% of my tithes
every month. And God bless me with good
health. Healthy family, food, clothes, a place
to live. (I still have test like (JOB in The Holy
Bible but we created in God likeness and image.
God blesses me and all my family to prevail, and
endure until the test is passed. We God children.
We will endure unto the end.

(54) JEREMIAH 3 Verse 12

Go and proclaim these words toward the north, and say
Return, thou backsliding Israel, (P35) saith the LORD;
and I will not cause mine anger to fall upon you; for I am
merciful, saith the LORD, and I will not keep anger for
ever. "Stop sinning today! Amen

(55) MATTHEWS Verse 34

But I say unto you, swear not at all; neither by heaven; for
it is God throne. Amen

(If you swear stop). Amen

(56) MATTHEWS Verse 41

And whosoever shall compel thee to go a mile, go with
him twain. Amen

(Do this go the twain and the mile. Amen)

(57) MATTHEW 5 Verse 42

Give to him that asketh thee, and from him that would borrow of thee turn not thou away. Amen

Give what you can. When you can. When you don't have it you can not give. Until God bless you with more to keep giving.

(Get this)! Let this sink in your ears.

LUKE 6
Verse 35

But love ye your enemies and do good, and lend, hoping for nothing again; and your reward shall be great, and ye shall be the children of the Highest; for he is kind unto the unthankful and to the evil.

♥ Be kind. Lend to people and do not expect to get it back from who you lend to. God will repay you. (Read) PROVERBS 19:17 Amen

(58) ACTS 20 Verse 35

I have shewed you all things, how that so laboring you ought to support the weak, and to remember the words of the Lord Jesus, how he said. It is more blessed to give than to recieve. Amen

'Do you desire the poor get rich by God Almighty and have to give to you. No. Give when you can.' Amen

MATTHEW:24 VERSE:42 Watch therefore :for ye no not what hour your LORD doth come.

For all creations pray for them in your prayer closet. Put olive oil on their forehead.

Go to dollar tree or whatever bible store you choose. Buy them a New Testement pocket bible so they can have something to read. Get one for yourself and family. Amen

And get a authorize KING JAMES VERSION Holy Bible. Amen

They cost 1.00 at Dollar Tree Get HARD Back. And you can so on line and get 1 case if you like, at Dollar Tree. Amen

"Now if you can" afford to give them meat and drink (soda) Koolaide. No wine or strong drink. God keep people warm not wine & strong drink. Give. Amen

Give God Almighty Word" (In Yahshua Name)
Jesus

(59) MATTHEW 23 Verses 9-10

And call no man your father upon the earth: for one is your Father which is in heaven. Amen

Neither be ye called masters: for one is your Master, even Christ, Amen

(60) MATTHEW 23 Verse 8

But be not ye called Rabbi for one is your Master even Christ: and all ye are brethren. Amen

(61) LUKE 10 Verse 5

… And into whatsoever house ye enter; first say, Peace be to this house. Amen
- Read LUKE 10) now.

(62) LUKE 10 Verse 27

And he answering said Thou shalt love the Lord thy God with all thy heart, and with all thy soul, and with all thy strength, and with all thy mind; and thy neighbour as thyself. Amen

Love God & Jesus with all thy heart soul strength and mind forever and your neighbours. And your self. Love all God creations forever, Amen

(63) MALACH 3 Verse 10

Bring ye all the tithes into the storehouse, that there may be meat in mine house, and prove me now herewith, saith the LORD of hosts, if I will not open you the windows of heaven, and pour you cut a blessing, that there shall not be room enough to recieve it.
Read MALACH 3 now. - DO NOT put it off read & learn now today. Amen

(64) PROVERBS 3 Verse 27

Withhold not good from them to whom it is due, when it is in the power of thine hand to do it. Amen
(Read verse 28 now)

> * Always keep a bible in your car, bathroom, bedroom. And help who you can. "And" when you can give.

NUMBERS 6
Verses 22-27 Amen

And the LORD spake unto Moses, saying

Speak unto Aaron and unto his sons, saying on this wise ye shall bless the children of Israel saying unto them.

The LORD bless thee, and keep thee:

The LORD make his face shine upon thee, and be gracious unto thee:

The LORD lift up his countenance upon thee, and give thee peace. Amen

Put a drop of olive oil on your forehead before you so to sleep. And when God wake you and your family up. Amen

(65) JAMES 5 Verse 14

Is any sick amoung you? Let him call for the elders of the church; and let them pray over him anointing him with oil in the name of the Lord. Amen

Keep olive oil in your medicine cabinet in your bathroom. Amen

(66)   No one will not make God Almighty word come back void.

> * All lies They the creations of God say because a child do not have their daddy in their home. That the children will end up in prisons. So creations of God thought to build more prisons instead of building houses, manisons, palaces.

For the simple fact we all the children of the Most High God. And it is written in PSALM 82. Amen

{Here is God Almighty Promise.
JOHN 8
Verse 47

He that is of God heareth God's words: Ye therefore hear them not, because ye are not of God. Amen}

(67)   God Almighty bless us all to hear his words.

1 JOHN 5
Verse 14

(And this is the confidence that we have in him, that, if we ask any thing according to his will, he heareth us. Amen Amen Amen)

(68) JOHN 17 Verse 15

> I pray not that thou shouldest take them out of the world, but that thou shouldest keep them from the evil. Amen

Jesus prayed for us that's why we reformed, and been increasing more and more. Because we blessed of the LORD. Jesus prayed for us. You know those prayers are answered. Amen Amen Amen Amen

> * Our children grandchildren and all our generations & kinfolks & friends going just where God blessed us to pray. We going to church and we going to have church in our homes everyday all day and night. You want to know how. Read DEUTERONOMY Chapter 6, and DEUTERONOMY Chapter 11 verses 19 to 27 and PROVERBS 22 verse 6. Amen

Keep the prisons and jails and projects. And for once in your life. Use God Almighty money wisely. Amen - No to more prisons, jails, and project homes
You had money to build more jails and prisons. Then you get money to build poor, needy and all poor prisoners and felons a brand new apartment or house.

(69) In DEUTERONOMY 14. THE WORD OF God teach all people. To eat clean foods. Like

(a) Beef
(b) Turkey
(c) Chicken
(d) Perch
(e) Whiting

(f) Talopia

Amen

(Not) unclean foods

(h) pork
(i) shrimp
(j) catfish
(k) crablegss

Amen

Read DEUTERONOMY 14.

(70) LEVITICUS 3 Verse 17

It shall be a perpetual statute for your generations throughout all your dwellings, that ye eat neither fat nor blood.
- Do not eat fat or blood. Amen

(71) LEVITICUS 18 Verse 6

None of you shall approach to any that is near of kin to him to uncover their nakedness; I am the LORD. Amen
Read LEVITICUS 18

(72) LEVITICUS 18 Verse 22

Thou shalt not lie with mankind, as with womankind; it is abomination.

- Men do not marry or date men.
- Women do not marry or date a woman. Amen

(73) LEVITICUS 22 Verse 24

Ye shall not offer unto the LORD that which is bruised or crushed, or broken, or cut; neither shall ye make any offering thereof in your land. Amen

(74) Jesus never celebrated Christmas or no man made pasen holiday. Amen

JEREMIAH 10
Verse 3

For the customs of the people are vain: for one cutteth a tree out of the forest, the work of the hands of the workman with the ax. Amen
- (Read all of (JEREMIAH 10)

LUKE 2
Verses 41-42

Now his parents went to Jerusalem every year at the feast of the Passover. Amen

And when he was tweleve years, old they went up to Jerusalem after the custom of the feast. Amen
PS. Jesus celebrated the Passover and Feasts of the LORD. It is written

"THE FEASTS OF"
THE LORD

(75) JOHN 7 Verse 14

Now about the midst of the feast Jesus went up into the temple and taught. Amen

(76) LEVITICUS 23 Verses 1-2

And the LORD spake unto Moses, saying

Speak unto the children of Israel, and say unto them, concerning the feasts of the LORD which ye shall proclaim to be holy convocations, even these are my feasts. Amen

(77) You know good and well Sunday (is not) the Sabbath Day or 7th day. "From sunset every Friday to sunset every Saturday (is) the TRUE Sabbath Day. Read HEBREWS 4

(78) HEBREWS 4 Verses 9-10

There remaineth therefore a rest to the people of God. Amen

For he that is entered into his rest, he also hath ceased from his own works, as God did from his. Amen

(79) GENESIS 2 Verse 2

And on the seventh day God ended his work which he had made; and he rested on the seventh day from his work which he had made. Amen

Rest sunset (every Friday) to (Sunset every Saturday).

(80) EXODUS 16 Verse 23

And he said unto them. This is that which the LORD hath said Tomorrow is the rest of the holy Sabbath unto the LORD; bake that which ye will bake to day, and seethe that ye will seethe; and that which remaineth over lay up for you to be kept until the morning. Amen

Cook enough food on Fridays for Saturdays. Cook plenty for everybody living at your home. And for whoever gonna be there. Read EXODUS 16 Amen

(81) EXODUS 20 Verse 11

For in six days the LORD made heaven and earth, the sea and all that in them is, and rested the seventh day: wherefore the LORD blessed the Sabbath day and hallowed it. Amen
(Rest)

(82) MATTHEW 12 Verse 36

(But I say unto you, that every idle word that men shall speak they shall give account thereof in the day of judgment. Amen)

Do not use these words period.

(83) MATTHEW 18 Verse 1

How think ye? If a man have an hundred sheep, and one of them be gone astray, doth he not leave the ninety and nine, and goeth into the mountains, and seek that which is gone astray. Amen

** Go bring your lost children home. And pray with & for them (In Jesus Name).
Lost as in runaways and lost spiritually, or homeless. Amen

(84) LUKE 17 Verse 10

(So likewise ye, when ye shall have done all those things which are commanded you say, we are unprofitable servants: we have done that which was our duty to do. Amen)

(No matter who you help. You doing your duty! Amen)

(85) PROVERBS 22 Verse 6

(Train up a child in the way he should go; and when he is old, he will not depart from it. Amen

Train them to put and always love God and Jesus first and the most. Train them to always go to church every week. And obey God WORD. Amen)

(86) PROVERBS 21 Verse 17

(He that loveth pleasure shall be a poor man; he that loveth wine and oil shall not be rich. Amen)

(87) PROVERBS 22 Verse 24

(Make no friendship with an angry man; and with a furious man thou shalt not go. Amen)

(88) PROVERBS 20 Verse 22

(Say not thou, I will recompense evil; but wait on the LORD and he shall save thee. Amen)

(89) Never light your oven on the Sabbath Day! Amen

EXODUS 35
Verse 3

Ye shall kindle no fire throughout your habitations upon the Sabbath day. Amen

*Do not light your stove (oven).

(90) EXODUS 31 Verse 13

Speak thou also unto the children of Israel, saying, verily my Sabbaths ye shall keep; for it is a sign between me and you throughout your generations; that ye may know that I am the LORD that doth sanctify you. Amen

Keep the Sabbath Holy on Saturday instead of Sunday. Amen

My church phone number

(219) 979-2633

My church name Israel the Church of Jesus.

<u>Wed</u>/Question and Answer night

<u>Fridays</u>/Sabbath Lesson

<u>SAT</u>/Sabbath Lesson/GOD WORD

www.thykingdomcome7.com

(91) LUKE 2 Verse 8 tell us the season Jesus was born.

And there were in the same country shepherds abiding in the field, keeping watch over their flock by night. Amen

(92) NEHEMIAH 13 Verse 15

In those days saw I in Judah some treading winepresses on the Sabbath, and bringing in sheaves and lading asses; as also wine, grapes, and figs, and all manner of burdens, which they brought into Jerusalem on the Sabbath day: and I testified aganist them in the day wherein they sold victuals. Amen

(93) Follow peace with all men. Read (<u>HEBREWS 12 verse</u> 14).

Amen

(94) Obey them that have the rule over you. Read HEBREWS 13 verse 17 Amen

(95) Do not sin willfully

Read HEBREWS 10 verse 26 Amen

(96) Be careful how you treat strangers.

HEBREWS 13 verse 2. Amen

(97) Speak not evil one of another (EPEHSIANS 4) Amen

(98) Stop mummering. Stop complaining. Amen

(99) Stop disrespecting God Yahshua (Jesus) Amen

> (a) your parents
> (b) kinfolks
> (c) neighbours
> (d) teachers
> (e) preachers
> (f) police
> (g) bosses all creations.
> (h) authorities. Amen

(100) Live for God.

> (a) Go to church every time the church is open for service. Amen
> (b) Go to work and come straight home. Amen
> (c) Bring your check home. Amen
> (d) Pay God his tithes offering and put something in the basket of church for the poor. Amen
> (e) Pay your bills where you live. Amen
> (f) You have child support pay that. Amen
> (g) Buy your food. Amen
> (h) Dine and shop when you can afford to. Amen

(101) Get out of gangs. Amen

(102) Do not join gangs. Amen

(103) Go to church instead of clubs. Amen

(104) Do not argue. Amen

(105) Do not cuss. Amen

(106) Do not fuss. Amen

(107) Do not fight. Amen

(108) Do not forget to pray evening morning and at noon. Do not forget to read your bible with your family day and night. Do not forget while you living and obeying God Almighty. He keeping his promises. To bless you for obeying him. (In Yahshua Name) Amen.

By Sister Patricia Inez Sandifer (Born and raised in the merciful) praying city Gary Ind

We ought to obey God rather than man. Support the weak. Give to the poor including felons. Give the felons all felons section 8 with all utilities includeded food stamps a check Medicad. And a authorize King James Version Holy Bible, while you train them with a good paying permant job. And make these landlords lower their rent and paint and fix up these places. Paint the entire building every time someone move in a out. Amen.

THE END
1st Book

P.S.

At all pantries let the poor wait inside instead of in the cold and heat, feed them meat and drink while they wait. Jimmine Dean Turkey Crossiant & Juice

Let poor include all felons rides buses free. Like the college students. Give elders their own buses.

They about to get that God Almighty heaven sent record deal. Call us
- (a) (219) 964-7219
- (b) (765) 237-4105
- (c) (219) 318-9454
- (d) (219) 951-7710

I have a son that rap Reggie I call him Faith.

Reggie son Rapp. Has name Lil Reggie

Reggie daughters rap Regenie and Rakelle, Reginie also draw.

My oldest daughter Laitarsha rap and her son Kendall.

I have grandsons that desire to play pro basketball. Give us a call.
- (a) (219) 964-7219
- (b) (765) 237-4105
- (c) (219) 318-9454
- (d) (219) 951-7710

Kendall is hot. Timothy is hot. Lil Reggie is hot. Brandon hot Kenny hot Garnette hot, Yashar, Lil Dave, T, Eric, Baby Garrette, Amari, and Cardea hot. These God and Jesus boys. If you hear any noise. It is just God and his boys dunkin shooting dribbling, passing that ball. Play ball. Give them a call. We waiting.

My grandson (Brother) Timothy Sandifer IV from Gary Indiana was staying with me (1) year. When God Almighty and Jesus Christ wake him up. God have him to pray without being told. Then he read his bible. Listen to the gospel. Then God start his day.

So I came to my grandson Timothy one day and said. Timothy you do your prayer, read God word, listen to the gospel, pay your tithes. And Timothy share his money with the poor. Whenever he go to the store. He see someone poor. He buy them something. So I told him take this ink pen and paper. And write what you want on this paper.

And he made these cartoons.

This is Timothy talking to his Brother Brandon again.

Brandon, Brandon, Brandon. What did God say in (Luke 1: Verse 35). The authorize King James Version Holy Bible?

This Timothy talking to Brandon about the way the truth the life.

Brandon, Brandon, Brandon, you know good well. You not suppose to turn that game on before you pray, read your bible, and listen to the gospel on the radio. Repent for the Kingdom of heaven is at hand.

"This is Brandon Repenting"

Lord I'm a sinner. Will you forgive me for turining the game on? "Im so very sorry for all the wrong things I do, like eating pork, shrimp, catfish, crabless, and for turning the game on our Father which art in heaven. Hallowed be thy name, thy kingdom come, thy will be done on earth as it is in heaven. Give us this day our daily bread, and forgive us our debts, as we forgive our debtors and lead us not into temptation but deliver us from evil for thine is the kingdom the power and the glory forever amen.

This is Tomothy

Daddy and Mother say, we got to read the book Exodus. Read 1 hour in the day. And 1 hour at night. Cause you know our Heavenly father said to keep the Pass over this Sping Amen Brandon. (Exodus 12)

Exodus 13

"This is Brandon."

Amen Timothy Amen. You know our Heavenly father is so blessed. And I thank him for giving us *The Feasts Days. As well as *The Entire Bible. So he can have us to be holy as he is holy forever ("In Yahshua Name")

The is Brandon listening to God word on the radio "In that last day that great day of the feast. Jesus stood and cried saying. If any man thirst let him come unto me and drink. Amen.

"Meditate" . . . .
(Joshua 1 Verse 8)

"Pray". . . . . . .
(Psalm 55 Verse 8)

This is Brandon.
Reading his bible.

This is Brandon playing the game.

Teach your children to put God first. By, having them to pray, read a bible verse, and have them to listen to (I) Chapter per day and night. (Began in Genesis If God permit) Before playing the game! Amen)

I thanks you for time.

By: Timothy Nataniel Sandifer IV
(read Psalm 112)
If God permit.

Born and raised in Gary Ind.

Timothy Parents:

- Daddy — Timothy N. Sandifier III
- Mother — Britney Wade
- Sister — Cherish Sandifier
- Brothers — Brandon and Cardea

To those that are interest dial (219) 318-9454

If God permit my dream for Timothy is that God Almighty and Jesus Christ.

Put Timothy work in

(a) Newspapers
(b) on Milk cartons
(c) on Meat packages
(d) on Benches
(e) on Bill Boards
(f) on T-shirts
(g) on Napkins, paper cups etc.

(Jeremiah 32: verse 27)

My grandon Timothy desire to own a bank one day. If God permit

* For with God nothing shall be impossible

(Luke 1:37)
(Psalm 34:10)
(Psalm 89)
(Psalm 112)

* To those that are interested cal: (219) 318-9454 (765) 237-4105 (219) 951-7710 (219) 964-7219

Amen

I thank you for your time.

By Timothy Sandifer IV
Born and raised in Gary Ind.
My parents are Timothy Nathanel Sandifer III and Brittney Wade.

I have 2 brothers and 1 sister

Brandon my brother
Cherish my sister
Cardea my brother.

My dream for Timothy is to one day have his cartoons in newspapers all over God Almighty and Jesus Christ earth. And I desire to watch the newspapers pay him for using his cartoons.

Timothy want to own a bank one day to help the poor
If you are interested in his cartoons. Call

Tim	(219) 318-9454
Tarsha	(219) 237-4105
Janel	(219) 951-7710
Ressie	(219) 964-7219

1 SAMUEL 12
Verses 7-8

The LORD maketh poor, and maketh rich; he bringeth low he lifeth up

He raiseth up the poor out of the dust, and lift up the beggar from the dunghill to set them amoung princes, and to make them inherit the throne of glory; for the pillars of the earth are the LORD'S and he hath set the world upon them

PSALMS 145:14 verse 15

The LORD upholdeth all that fall, and raiseth up all those that be bowed down

The eyes of all wait upon thee; and thou givest them their meat in due season.

PSALMS 146:8

The LORD open the eyes of the blind; the LORD raiseth them that are bowed down; the LORD loveth the righteous

(91) DEUTERONOMY 11 Verses 19-20

And ye shall teach them your children, speaking of them when thou sittest in thine house, and when thou walkest by the way, when thou liest down, and when thou risest up. Amen

And thou shalt write them upon the door posts of thine house and upon thy gates. Amen

(92) JEREMIAH 17 Verse 22

Neither carry forth a burden out of your houses on the Sabbath day, neither do ye any work, but hallow ye the Sabbath day, as I command your fathers, Amen

Call someone on the Sabbath for any emergency you may have. Amen

Thine will be done on earth as it is in heaven
Turn your back on your other gods and evil way

God made your daughter a female.

Read...
LEVITICUS
Chapter 18
Versezz
Amen

"In Yesus Name
✗ By Kendall Johnson
Yust call me Yudse
Kendall. One day I'll be your Yudse.

• Do not allow her to say she a male

God made your son a male never let him say he a female.

Read:
2LEVITICUS 18
Versezz

"In Yesus Name
By Kendall
Johnson. Yust
call me Yudse Kendall.
One day I will be your
Yudse. If God permit

It is maddness that man made up.

God Almighty made you a male. Be who God made you to be.
In "Jesus" Name. Amen

Lion

Lamb

turtle

male
boy

By: Rachel
Sandifer

God Almighty made you a female. Be who God made you to be in "Jesus" Name. Amen

Remember

No one know the day or the hour that our LORD shall return. Will you be ready.

Or will you still be lying to get what you want.

Or stealing and talking smart to your parents because you an adult now.

Will you still be making a fool out of yourself. Aurguing, fighting,

You know, for yourself Jesus never did any of those things.

So straighten yourself up. And do what you suppose to do.

You got a problem with someone. Let God and Jesus know. They will fight and battles for you. As long as you tell them the truth concerning what you going through.

Do not take the mark of the beast. But my God shall supply all our need according to his riches in glory in Christ Jesus. Stop judging people thinking it is only hope for you and your loved ones.

Nothing is too hard for God, dear prisoners, dear poor and needy people & creations.

There is hope for your Mr. Dope man. Put down your dope. And go to God and Jesus house the church. Go every time the door of the church is open.

Be ready to hear God Word.

Be ready to do what God Word say.

Pay your tithes 10% of all God give you.

Give what you can for an offering. What you can afford.

Give a offering to the poor too. What you can afford.

Go to church.

Go to work on times. Leave 2 hours early in winter. 1 hour early year round. In case you have to get some fast food, get your gas in the evening.

"Let God Almighty show" you the good in Gary Ind.

PROVERBS 19
Verse 4

"Wealth maketh many friends, but the poor is separated from his neighbor."

"In Gary Ind. some people say there is no work."

There is work in Gary Ind. And on the entire earth. Put God first and teach his gospel. That's work Gary Ind. Put God first. In Gary Ind. The important thing parents and grandparents teach the children is about God and Jesus. That is work.

They don't wait until they are 30. They teach them at birth.

Gary people teach and take the children to church.

To you. It don't seem like nothing going on in Gary Ind.

But God, Jesus and I know better.

*There is something going on for all to know.

Gary Ind. About God Almighty business giving to the poor.

And helping and caring for one another, helping their fellow brother.

And in Gary Ind. They loving their neighbor as there self.

Listen to what God said. He that hath pity upon the poor. Lend unto the LORD; And that which he giveth will God pay again.

And all Gary houses, children grandchildren & family. Give to the poor in Gary Ind.
The young and the elders. Give no matter who have a need in Gary Ind.

They give what they can. You don't even have to say please. In Gary. On 9th and Broadway. And 21st and Virginia. God so mighty. God get his people young and elders giving. You short of a penny nickle dime quater, dollar Gary Ind givers. You need a penny they giving not lending giving you. A penny nickle, dime, or quarter. Even a whole dollar or more, when they can.

In the stores, on the bus, at school. Wherever Gary Indiana people see a need. They do their duty. And give what they can that is God Almighty plan.

At some of their grocery stores. They give rides. It may cost some dollars. But that there also please our heavenly Father.

A servant is worthy of thy hire. Pay thy servant.

That's what you call power from the Most High God. Using your cars to give the poor a ride, give helping our heavenly Abba (Father) poor, is a joy

They never asked to be poor. So let's follow God steps that's why he made each one of us for.

To give to the poor. Ye gonna always have the poor in the land. And he that give to the poor (shall not) lack, but he that hide his eyes shall have many a curse.

Let that be your verse to keep in your purse so open up your purse & wallets.

Sisters, brothers, rich, people teacher, doctors, lawyers judges, police, firemen ect. … In all places and all races. Put smile on your faces and let's do our duty like Christ in Gary Ind making things better and better. That's what God asked of us. And all will be ok. All will be well. Amen Amen

By Sister Patricia Inez Sandifer

To all Gary Indiana the heares and doers of the word of God. Keep helping God poor. Yall keep helping and loving one another Gary Ind ye one blessed. Praise the LORD Gary Ind peace be unto you. What's up. Thanks for buying my book.

PSALMS 34
Verse 1

The Authorize King James
Version Holy
Bible

I will bless the LORD at all times: his praise shall continually be in my mouth.
Amen

PSALMS 34
Verse 19

Many are the afflictions of the righteous: but the LORD delivereth him out of them all.
Amen

PSALMS 71
Verse 8

Let my mouth be filled with thy praise and with thy honour all the day. Amen.

1 CORINTHIANS 11
Verses 4 and 5

Every man praying or prophesying, having his head covered dishonoureth his head.
Amen

*Males (never) cover your head when you pray or prophesying
Amen

But every women that prayeth or prophesieth with her head uncovered dishonoureth her heads for that is even all one as if she were shaven.

*Females babies females too. (Always cover your head when praying a prophesying) Amen

(PSALMS 115
Verses 14-15)

THE AUTHORIZE KING JAMES VERSION
Holy Bible

The LORD shall increase you more and more, you and your children Amen

Ye are blessed of the LORD which made heaven and earth. Amen

(PSALMS 82
Verse 6)

I have said, ye ar gods, and all of you are children of the Most High Amen.

(JOHN 15
Verse 3)

Now ye are clean through the word which I have spoken unto you. Amen

(JOHN 17
Verse 8)

For I have given unto them the words which thou gavest me, and they have received them, and have known surely that I came out from thee, and they have believed that thou didst send me. Amen

(JOHN 17 Verse 11)

And now I am no more in the world, but these are in the world, and I come to thee. Holy Father, keep through thine own name those whom thou hast given me, that they may be one as we are one. Amen

(1 JOHN 5
Verses 14-15)

And this is the confidence that we have in him, that if we ask any thing according to his will, he heareth us. Amen

And if we know that he hear us, whatsoever we ask, we know that we have the petitions that we desired of him. Amen.

*Lord I'm a sinner. Will you forgive me and all sinners, now thank you for hearing these prayers.

EXODUS 20
Verse 12

Honour thy father and thy mother: that thy days may be long upon the land which the LORD thy God giveth thee.

They shared their God Jesus, their love, their faith, their home, their money. No matter how grown we were. They say if you ever need to come home. Our room and bed will always be there "Mr & Mrs Clifton and Clearce" (Sandifer) Sr, are our parents.

MATTHEW 23:9

And call no man your father upon the earth: for one is your Father which is in heaven.

*My daddy say do not call me Father call me Daddy.

God have young men everywhere that dress and wear their hair different ways. They may be on street corners where ever they be in clubs, pubs. But they love God Almighty and Jesus Christ. Thank you Brother Mario

This young man and his fiance love Jesus. One day I was passing out the Ten Commandments free to people. And my children always tease me and say, ma these people you trying to give these Ten Commandments to. Gonna say, Lady I don't know you. My children be just playing and teasing with me.

This young man Brother Mario was so glad to have God Ten Commandment him and his fiance. That's why God say man don't see how God see. Man look on the outward apperance but God look at the heart. Bless you. Bless you.

Deuteronomy 14

Both my parents Mr. & Mrs. Clifton & Clearece Sandifer Sr. Born & raised in Jackson and McComb Miss. And lived in Gary Ind.

My parents Clifton & Clearece Sandifer Sr. Born in Jackson & McComb Miss. Lived in Gary Ind. also.

My mother Clearece Allen Sandifer McGee.

My mother Clearece Allen Sandifer McGee.

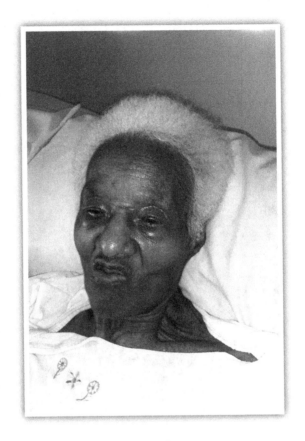

My mother Clearece Allen Sandifer McGee.

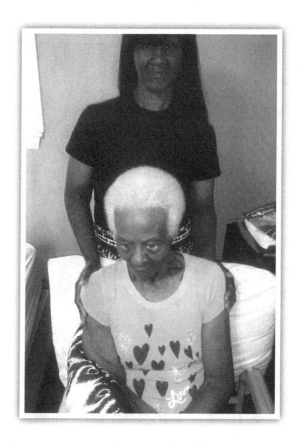

Myself. Sister Patricia and my mother Clearece Allen Sandifer McGee.

My nephew, Antione Lemonte Howard.

This is sister Patricia the author of this book.

This is sister Patricia the author of this book praising the Lord before I go to work.

This is sister Patricia Inez Sandifer meditating

This is sister Patricia

This is sister Patricia

This is sister Patricia and her youngest daughter Janel Johnson graduating from nursing school.

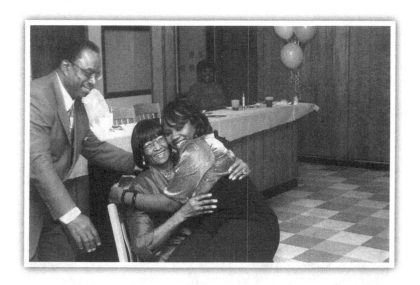

This is my oldest daughter. In my mother lap. And my brother Glenn a school teacher. My sister in law Felicia in the back.

(My oldest daughter La' Tasha) is owner of Kenny Kendall Gourmet Popcorn. Atlanta she just moved to your city. Get some of that good popcorn. And good lemonade.

*For popcorn (765) 532-9241
**You can order your popcorn anywhere in the world. And it will be delivered in the mail

This is my mother Clearece McGee with my youngest daughter Janel Johnson. Janel is a nurse. My mother was a semstress that sewed for the mayor, judges, lawyer, teachers, neighbors, family friends.

My mother with my oldest son. My mother Clearece McGee. My oldest son Timothy Nathaniel Sandifer. Tim wants to watch God & Jesus move your snow. And keep your lawn holy & lovely. Tim have a lawn care and snow removal business. Give him a call all business. Lafayette & West Lafayette.

Tim (219) 3189454
* Corporate Business & all business in Laf & West Laf. Give my son a call. Peace!

This is my mother Clearece, with my youngest son Reginald Danyale Sandifier Sr. Ressie is a rapper. He is a good as, Lil Wayne, Jay-Z, Snoop, Kanya, and Will Smith. My son Reginold also go all over God and Jesus earth restoring houses. He work in Resteration. He's going to buy me a houses with a chandeler soon as God and Jesus get that Huge Record Deal. (In <u>Yahshua</u> Name)

Jesus

If the Lord will we shall live we shall do this as that. My son Rapper name is Reginelli Mega-Don Carleon. My son don't just desire a record deal. He desire to help the poor even more. He do what he can for any poor person no matter what relegion or color. No matter what city he in.

One day his children and I and Reggie was about to go out and eat.

My son Reggie get a phone call as we were going in the restaurant.

He handed me his card. He took his phone call in his car. And me and his children went in the restaurant. As we were about to order. There stood a poor man. As we ordered our food. We ordered the poor man what he wanted. Because that's what God Almighty, Jesus Christ and Reggie would have done for the poor man.

My mother Clearece. My nephew Antione and A PRAYER HE WROTE the day he was gunned down in his home.

Thank you Lord for everything you've done for me. Forgive me of all my sins. BE the Lord of my life. Create in me a clean heart and a right spirit in me. Renew my mind. HEAL ME FROM THE HURT OF MY PAST..(I LOVE AND NEED YOU). Cover me with your precious and Holy Blood as well as my family, my friends. And all my lifes projects. Give me your dreams. LORD Bless and protect everyone that seek you and believe in you.*** No one has been arrested.

My daughter in red Janel.
My son Reginald in the middle
My daughter Tarsha in black

Left to right.
My youngest son Reginald that I call Faith.

In the middle, my grandson Garrette. I call Believe

My oldest son Tim that I call Goodness.

I got their nicknames out the Holy Bible.

My Grandson Kendall praising Dreadful the Great King

Dreadful is God Almighty "In Yahshua Name")
                                        Jesus.

Kendall is going to be a lawyer and judge one day. He loving helping the poor.

In the middle in black my youngest daughter Janel

On the right standing white blouse. My granddaughter Alize Smith

In the very front my grandson white shirt Yashar Johnon. Yashar & his brother Garrett desire to play for the white Sox.

My oldest son Tim with his children Timothy Sandifer white Shirt Brandon Sandifer black shirt, Cherish Sandifer white blouse French braids.

Cherish & Brandon desire to be surgeons that pray over people according to James S. Timothy desire to own banks to help the poor.

This is my grandson Reginald Sandifer Jr.

Reginald desire to be a professional basketball player.
Give as a call. 219 9647219   219 9517710   765 2374105
219 3186454

This is my grandaughter Regena Sandifer

She raps.
She draws.
She want a deal with you. Give her dad a call. Big Reggie (Faith)
is her dad
(219) 964 7219

Baby (Brook Smith)
Janel granddaughter
Brook daddy is Garrette Smith with my mother Clearece

My oldest daughter Tarsha/Joy
Owner of Kenny Kendall Gourmet Popcorn.
With my Grandson Garrette III.

* Snoop, Lil Wayne, Will & Jade Smith, Kanya & Kim, Jayz &
All yall family get same popcorn!
Good ole Cheeder Cheesey Yummy. Hot popcorn
Oh my God. So many flavors. Give them a call for popcorn
(765) 532-9241

Left to right
My youngest son Reginald that I call Faith

Middle person. Mark my nephew I call OBADIAH

Right my oldest son Timothy I call Goodness. I got their nicknames out the Holy Bible.

Alize Smith (Stanley) my granddaughter, and Tyreasa Havard
my niece. She is a Nutrionist. Snoop, Lil Wayne Jayz Will
Kanya and all yall family & friends. She want to be your
Give her a call (219) 334-8800
And on the right is my niece Tyresa.

Zeze in the white my niece. Her real name Azisha Sease.

Her mother in the black Mildred Sease.

Zeze is a boss over a very big company. She's a young good boss.

Mildred is a public defender. And she know how to do her job well.

From left to right

My nephew in black
(Torey Howard) He is in college.

My nice in middle
(Tyreasa Howard)

My nephew in white
TJ. (Antione Howard)
He is college.

This is Heaven (the dog name Heaven) Antione my nephew dog.

This dog watched someone gun down my nephew in his own home.

God & Jesus know who killed him. The hidden will be revealed.

This is my nephew Wilton Sandifer (PJ).

PJ drive for Uver.

Pam Mary (my sister) friend with my mother.

Pam be a friend that stick closer than a brother.

This is my sister Mary friends

Pam and her husband.

Cheryl   Mary my sister friend who also was by my sister side. When my sister son was killed.

This is Sister Patricia & Brother Andrea taking a picture. We were out sharing with the poor one rainey rainey day.

Printed in the United States
by Baker & Taylor Publisher Services